ISBN 978-0-9839288-0-5

CONTENTS

USING A FAMILY DEVOTION

Pray, pray, pray. Begin your family devotion in thoughtful prayer. Pray that God will use this devotion to change the lives of you and your family. Follow the daily schedule. If you miss a day, don't worry. Just pick up where you left off. Relax and enjoy your family. It is designed for thirty days, but if it takes longer, great. Our goal is for this to be a lifelong plan. It's time with your family and that is our goal.

Read the scripture and commentary to your family. Then ask the questions that are supplied and start the discussions as the Holy Spirit leads. Give your family time to think about an answer before you move on. Do not get frustrated and do not get discouraged, this will take time to master. Just stick with it. Man Up! and let's start raising a godly generation.

So, if you are wondering what you are going to do after the thirty days are over, don't. At the end of this booklet, there is a website address for you to download more days for your family devotions. Finish these 30 days and then move on. Our prayer is that starting now, you will be building Christ centered homes and healthy habits for you and your family.

God Bless,
Man Up! Gods Way

Visit us at
www.manupgodsway.org

INTRODUCTION:

The purpose of this booklet is to build Christ-Centered Homes and strengthen foundations so that we can fulfill the Great Commission. In this booklet you will begin to follow the life of Christ.

Our prayer is that you will use this booklet as a daily devotional for the next thirty days with your family. As the family goes, so goes the church. Our churches, communities and nations are only as strong as our families.

Deuteronomy 6:4-7 (NKJV) 4 "Hear, O Israel: The Lord our God, the Lord is one! 5 You shall love the Lord your God with all your heart, with all your soul, and with all your strength. 6 "And these words which I command you today shall be in your heart. 7 You shall teach them diligently to your children, and shall talk of them when you sit in your house, when you walk by the way, when you lie down, and when you rise up".

You see, we are commanded to teach these (God's commands) to our children. Every moment with our children should be a teaching moment. Moses was telling the children of Israel to spend time with their children teaching them the ways of the Lord. Our job as fathers is the same; to teach them God's ways.

It is not the responsibility of the Sunday school teacher. Our job is to raise up children who know the Lord, who put the Lord first and who share the Lord everywhere they go (Matthew 28:18-20). Before we can rightly and biblically raise our children we must first determine, each day, who we will serve. Each morning when the day dawns, as we go to the Lord in prayer, we must be steadfast in our desire to serve Him only. Then as men we must be unmovable in our love and devotion to our families and teach them the word of God.

After many nights of frustrating family devotions, I began to try to write my own devotion for my family. I was looking to write something that was engaging, thought provoking and fun for my children. But nothing ever came to mind and I just couldn't put on paper what my heart felt my family needed. I began to search the internet for something that might help us and discovered a daily devotional for families at the website of the ministry of Heaven's Family (**www.heavensfamily.org/ss/devotionals**). I began doing these with my family and realized there was no reason to reinvent the wheel. I contacted David Servant and asked if Man Up! Gods Way Ministries could use his family devotions. He was gracious enough to allow us to create a family devotions booklet for men to take into their homes. We are thankful for his ministry and we know you will be to.

Jody Burkeen
Man Up! Ministries

ABOUT DAVID SERVANT

David Servant has served in vocational ministry for over thirty years as a pastor, author and international teacher. He is the author of eight books and has ministered God's Word in over fifty nations. Apart from Jesus, he is nothing. He resides in Pittsburgh, Pennsylvania with his wife, Rebecca. They are the parents of three adult children and the grandparents of one delightful little boy named Liam.

MAN UP GODS WAY MINISTRIES

Jody Burkeen is the Founder of Man Up! Gods Way Ministries, pastor, speaker and author of Man Up! Becoming a Godly Man in an Ungodly World. He has been married for 21 years and has two children ages 9 and 10. He currently resides in St. Louis, Missouri.

The Pre-Existence and Deity of Christ
John 1:1-3; 17:5, 24

The story of Jesus begins long before He was born as a baby in Bethlehem. Because Jesus is and always has been God's Son, He existed before anyone or anything was created. John wrote that Jesus was with God "in the beginning" (John 1:2), which means before the world was created and before time began. When Jesus was conceived in Mary's womb, He was not created---He just moved from heaven to earth and changed His form into a tiny human being inside Mary's belly. It would be something like shrinking and transforming yourself into an ant in order to visit an ant colony.

Not only was Jesus *with* God in the beginning, but John also said that Jesus *was* God. There are three persons who, according to the Bible, can be called God: God the Father, God the Son (Jesus) and God the Holy Spirit. Jesus is just as much God as God the Father is God. We learned today that Jesus helped create everything that exists (see John 1:3).

We also read that Jesus prayed to God the Father just before He died, "Father, bring me into the glory we shared before the world began" (John 17:5). Before the world was created, Jesus lived in heaven, a place filled with God's glory, with His Father. What is God's glory? It is something like sunshine, only much brighter. It radiates from God.

The best part is that everyone who is a follower of Jesus will one day see God's glory in heaven, because Jesus requested that we would. He prayed, "Father, I want these whom you've given me [that includes us] to be with me [in heaven], so they can see my glory" (John 17:24). When we see Jesus one day in heaven, He'll be brightly shining with God's glory. The Bible tells us that His face will shine like the sun (see Matthew 16:27-17:2)!

Q. Where did God the Father, Son and Holy Spirit come from?

A. The answer is that They have always existed. They have no beginning and no end. That is hard for us to understand, but that is the answer. The reason we have difficulty understanding it is because most everything we know has a beginning and an end.

Q. Why did John call Jesus "the Word"?

A. The word *word* sometimes means "a message." For example, your teacher might say, "I have a word from our principal," meaning a message from the principal. Or you might hear someone on a TV show say, "And now a word from our sponsor," which means a commercial is coming with a message from an advertiser. Jesus is given many symbolic titles in the Bible, such as "Lamb," "Cornerstone" and so on, which all describe something He has done for us. Perhaps He is called "the Word" (or "the Word of God"; see Rev. 19:13) because Jesus was God's message to all people of the world. Isn't it amazing that God had a message prepared for all the people of the world even before He even created anyone?

Application: *Because we will one day live with Jesus in heaven and see His glory, we should live "in a manner worthy of the God who calls [us] into His own kingdom and glory"(1 Thessalonians 2:12, NASB).*

NOTES: *(Idea- Write down the answers your kids give for each of the questions. It will be fun to go back at later dates and see what they say.)*

The Deity and Humanity of Jesus Christ
John 1:14; Isaiah 7:14; 9:6

Yesterday we read what John wrote about Jesus being called "the Word." A few verses later in his Gospel, John said, "the Word [who is Jesus] became human and lived here on earth among us" (John 1:14). John was talking about when the glorious God Jesus was transformed into a baby in Mary's womb, lived there for nine months, was born, grew up, and lived for about 33 years on the earth as a human being. It was a really big miracle for God to become a man, but nothing is too hard for God!

It's very important for us to understand that Jesus was a very special person. He was God transformed into a man. He wasn't one-half human being and one-half God. He was 100% of both. That has not been the case with any other person who has ever lived. Jesus was one-of-a-kind! He wanted us to know that He was both human and divine, calling Himself the *Son of God* and the *Son of Man*.

Hundreds of years before Jesus became a man, God told Isaiah the prophet what He was planning to do. He promised that a special baby would be born through a woman who had never been married. People often have special names that they call their babies, such as "sweet pea," "little guy" or "chubby cheeks." But the special baby that God told Isaiah about would be called "Immanuel," a name that means "God is with us" (Isaiah 7:14). That is what Jesus was. He was no longer the God in heaven---He was God living with us.

Through Isaiah, God the Father helped us understand how His Son, who had no beginning, would have a beginning as a human being. He promised, "For a child is born to us, a son is given to us" (Isaiah 9:6). It was a human being, a *child* , who was born in Bethlehem, but the Father's *Son* was not born because He always existed. Thus, He was *given* .

Finally, notice Jesus was born *to us* and given *to us* . It was *for us* that He came because God loves us.

Q. Let's pretend that you wanted to show the dogs in your neighborhood how much you loved them. What would you do? If you had the power, would you be willing to change yourself into a baby dog inside its mother, live there for nine months, be born as a puppy and live for 33 years as a dog when you could have been enjoying life as a human being? You would really have to love dogs to do that! Jesus becoming a man was a bigger step down than for us to become dogs. Does that give you an idea of how much Jesus loves us?

A. Yup!

Q. Are there any other major religions in the world besides Christianity that can truly say they were begun by a human being who was actually God?

A. Nope!

Application: *Since Jesus is God, we should pay careful attention to what Jesus said and obey Him.*

NOTES:

One Reason Why Jesus Became a Human Being
John 1:18; Hebrews 1:1-3

Many people have wondered what God is like. They've looked at flowers, snowflakes, hummingbirds and rainbows and realized that God must be *very* smart and *very* powerful. The things He's made are amazing! And when people eat a crisp apple, sit by a warm fire on a cold day, or listen to musical instruments, they realize that all those wonderful things are made possible by God, and so He must also be very kind.

But knowing God through what He's made is somewhat like knowing an artist only through his paintings. How much more could you learn about that artist if you could actually meet him in person and be friends for a few years?

God wants us to know Him personally, and not just through what He has created. That is one reason that God sent Jesus to the earth. We read today, "No one has ever seen God. But his only Son, who is himself God, is near to the Father's heart; he has told us about him" (John 1:18). Nobody knew God the Father better than Jesus. They had lived together forever! In the original language in which John wrote, he said something like, "Jesus and God the Father were bosom buddies!"

Not only did Jesus know more than anyone else about God the Father, He also *acted* more like God the Father than anyone else. Have you ever heard the expression, "Like father, like son"? That was certainly true concerning Jesus and His Father. Jesus once said, "Anyone who has seen me has seen the Father!" (John 14:9). If we want to learn what God the Father is like, all we have to do is learn about Jesus. We read today, "Everything about [Jesus] represents God exactly" (Heb. 1:3). If God the Father had become a human being instead of Jesus, He would have said and done the same things.

Before Jesus came, there were only two ways to learn about God: through looking at His creation, and through studying the words of the people who wrote the Old Testament. Some of those people had experiences with God from which we can learn, and some of them (the prophets) actually spoke God's words. But ever since Jesus came, we now have three ways to learn about God! As we study the life and ministry of Jesus in the weeks ahead, we'll be learning about God, the creator of everything, a person with whom we'll be friends forever. What could be more exciting than that?

Q. Perhaps your parents are like most parents: one is a little more strict than the other. If you have to get a spanking, you probably would prefer to get it from your mother, because she doesn't spank quite as hard as your father! Do you think God the Father is more strict than Jesus is since He's the Father?

A. No. Both the Father and Son are equally loving and equally strict. They become equally angry over the same things and care about you the same.

Application: *Since God has put forth so much effort to help us to get to know Him, we should study His creation, His Word, and the life of Jesus so that He will become our closest friend.*

NOTES:

Another Reason Why Jesus Became a Human
1 Timothy 1:15; Hebrews 2:14-15

Yesterday we learned one reason why God's Son became a human being: to teach us about God. But there was a second reason that is even more important. Jesus became a human being so our sins could be forgiven, as we just read: "Christ Jesus came into the world to save sinners" (1 Timothy 1:15).

Why did Jesus have to come into the world in order for sinners to be saved? If God wanted to forgive sinners, why didn't He just do it from heaven? Why did God have to become a human being?

To answer those questions, we first have to understand something about God. He is perfect. He always does the right thing, and it wouldn't be right for God to simply forgive people who continually do bad and evil things. What would you think of your parents if they never punished a brother or sister who beat you up every day? You would think that they didn't love you and weren't fair.

If God didn't punish people when they did bad things, He would be unloving toward people who were hurt by other people's sins. And He would be acting unfairly. So God couldn't just decide not to punish people for their sins, or He would become a sinner Himself!

However, God loves the people He's created, and He needed a way to forgive them without becoming a bad person Himself. So God decided to become a human being who would face every temptation that anyone ever faced. He, however, would never sin. Then, as a substitute, He would take the punishment for everyone's sins! As an example: Perhaps you were about to be spanked for disobeying your mother or father, and your sister or brother volunteered to be spanked in your place! (Pretty slim chance of that happening, right?)

That is why God had to become a human being. God, of course, can't die, but humans can. So God became a human being in order to die. And His painful death was the payment for our sins. Jesus Himself said, "I...came here...to give my life as a ransom for many" (Mark 10:45). A ransom is a payment to set free someone who is a prisoner. Jesus gave His life as a payment to God's justice so He could set us free from our sins.

Q. Why couldn't some other human being have died for our sins instead of Jesus?

A. Because all of us have sinned, we all deserve to be punished. So none of us could serve as a substitute to die for the sins of others. It would be like two convicted murderers who become friends in prison. If both were sentenced to die in the electric chair, it would be silly for one to say to the prison warden, "I will sacrificially volunteer to die in place of my friend." The warden would reply, "You can't die for him because you are going to die for your own crime."

We needed someone who was sinless, who didn't deserve any punishment for his own sins, to be punished in our place. Jesus was the only person who has ever lived without sin.

Q. How could the painful death of only one person be enough payment for the many sins of everyone who has ever lived?

A. It was not the *amount* of suffering that made Jesus' death sufficient payment for everyone's sins; it was the fact of *who* did the suffering. Let's say, for example, that your dog attacked and killed your neighbor's dog. Your neighbor might demand that your dog be killed so that your dog suffers just as much as his did. That could be considered fair. But what if he demanded that *you* die for what your dog did? That would be unfair, because you are worth a lot more than a dog. You have more value than an animal!

In the same way, God has much more value than all the human beings put together. If Jesus had been *just* a man, His sufferings would have been sufficient payment for only one other person who deserved to die. But because God's value is infinitely higher than all human beings combined, His painful suffering was more than sufficient to be able to pay fairly for everyone's sins.

Application: *Since God loved us enough to die as our substitute, we should show Him love in return by doing what He says. Jesus said, "If you love me, obey my commandments"* (John 14:15).

NOTES:

The Birth of John the Baptist Foretold
Luke 1:5-25

This story happened about 2,000 years ago in Jerusalem, Israel. The Jewish people had a big building something like a church that was called the Temple. God had said that all the men who were descendants of Moses' brother, Aaron, were supposed to work at the Temple doing various jobs. They were called priests. One of their jobs was to burn incense, something that smelled very nice, in an inner room of the Temple, called "the holy place."

There were so many descendants of Aaron at the time of this story that they took turns doing the various jobs. It just happened that Zechariah was chosen to be the one to burn incense inside the Temple, and it was a once-in-a-lifetime opportunity for him. He was probably really excited to go in the Temple into a special room that few people ever got to see! Imagine how shocked he was when an angel named Gabriel suddenly appeared before him! Have you ever been scared in your own house when you suddenly saw a family member whom you didn't know was in the same room with you? Think of how you'd feel if it was someone you didn't recognize. What if it was someone who looked like an angel? No wonder Zechariah was "overwhelmed with fear" (Luke 1:12).

The angel told Zechariah some amazing news: In answer to his prayer, his elderly wife would have a special baby. Zechariah's son would be a great prophet and preacher, and by the Holy Spirit's power, he would persuade many people in Israel to quit sinning. That way, they would be prepared for another very special person who was about to come: God in the form of a man!

Zechariah didn't believe what he heard because he thought he and his wife were too old to have a baby. They were as old or older than your grandparents! But nothing is too hard for God, and

Zechariah should have believed what he heard. It was an angel who spoke to him, and that angel had just come from heaven to deliver the message from God.

God was a little bit angry with Zechariah's unbelief, so He took away Zechariah's ability to talk for about nine months! God expects us to believe what He says because He never lies. A lesson we can learn from Zechariah is that it is better to say nothing at all than to say something that disagrees with what God has said. God is always right in what He says.

Q. We learned today that many of the Israelite fathers weren't very good fathers, but when they heard John's preaching they repented and started to really show their kids that they loved them. What is the most important thing your father or mother could do to show you how much they love you?

A. Teach you about God and the Bible! (So you must have good parents!)

Q. When do you think Zechariah prayed to have a son?

A. Probably many years before when he was a younger man, since he didn't believe it was possible for his wife to have a baby even after hearing the angel's message. Our prayers are not always answered as soon as we'd like.

Application: *God's Word is always true, so we should never say anything that contradicts what God has said.*

NOTES:

DAY 6
Jesus' Birth Foretold to Mary
Luke 1:26-56

Back in the days of Elizabeth and Mary, people got married at a younger age than people do today, often when they were teenagers. Mary may have been only sixteen or so when the angel Gabriel appeared to her and told her she would have a child. Imagine God coming to the earth through a teenager!

Because she was not married to Joseph yet, Mary wondered out loud how she would be able to have a baby. Gabriel explained to her that although the baby would be *her* son, the child would not be Joseph's son. He would be *God's* son, conceived by the Holy Spirit. He would be the first and only God-man, 100% human and 100% God.

Gabriel told Mary that her son would be given the throne of His ancestor David and that He would "reign over Israel forever" (Luke 1:33). His kingdom would have no end. David was a great king who had ruled over the nation of Israel about one thousand years before the time of Jesus. When David was still alive God had promised him, "When you die, I will raise up one of your descendants....and I will establish the throne of His kingdom forever. I will be his father, and he will be my son....Your dynasty and your kingdom will continue for all time before me, and your throne will be secure forever" (2 Samuel 7:12-16). After David died, his descendants did rule after him for about five hundred years, but since then there has been no descendant of David ruling over Israel.

When Jesus lived on the earth He never did rule over Israel. In fact, the people of Israel killed Him. But God's promises are true. The Bible tells us that Jesus will one day live in Jerusalem, and from there He will rule the entire world! There won't be any United States of America then or any other countries---Jesus' kingdom will be the only kingdom. And His kingdom will never end! Everyone should want to be in that kingdom.

Gabriel told Mary that her relative Elizabeth had also experienced a miracle: she was pregnant in her old age. So Mary journeyed to Elizabeth's house and stayed with her for three months, probably until John was born. Elizabeth probably appreciated having someone to chat with during those three months since her husband couldn't talk!

When Mary arrived at Elizabeth's house, John, who was probably already filled with the Holy Spirit (see Luke 1:15), "jumped for joy" inside his mother. The Holy Spirit in John knew who was inside Mary, and was quite happy about it! So what is the key to being joyful? Being close to Jesus!

Elizabeth may have heard about what Gabriel had told Mary, because when Mary arrived at her door she already knew that Mary was pregnant with a very special child. Or it's possible that the Holy Spirit inspired her with a gift of prophecy, because we read that she was filled with the Holy Spirit upon Mary's arrival. Regardless, Elizabeth knew that Mary's baby was even more special than her own. She called Mary "the mother of [her] Lord" (Luke 1:43), so she knew that God was living inside Mary's womb.

It seems that Mary was suddenly filled with the Holy Spirit then as well, because she responded to Elizabeth's greeting by speaking a beautiful poem. It was all about God's goodness toward her and to everyone who fears Him. The best thing God did for us was to send Jesus! Like Mary, we're blessed!

Q. Because Mary and Elizabeth were somehow related, we know that Jesus and John the Baptist were distant relatives. Do you know of anyone who is alive today who is related to Jesus?

A. Everyone who believes and follows Jesus is a brother or sister of Jesus!

Q. Jesus lived inside of Mary for nine months. Has He ever lived inside of anyone else?

A. Yes! If you believe in Him, Jesus lives inside of you! He doesn't live inside you physically, like a baby inside its mother, but spiritually, because the Holy Spirit lives in everyone who believes in Jesus, and the Holy Spirit is just like Jesus and the Father. That is why Jesus once promised everyone who loves Him that both He and His Father would come to live inside them (see John 14:23).

Application: *Since Jesus lives in us by the Holy Spirit, we should always remember that He is with us to direct our thoughts, words and deeds.*

NOTES:

John the Baptist is Born
Luke 1:57-80

When new babies are born, people always make a fuss over them. If you've ever had a baby brother or sister born into your family, you may have felt like your mom and dad forgot about you for a little while. However, the fuss that was made over your baby brother or sister was nothing compared to the one that was made over John the Baptist when he was born. *Everybody* was talking about it for miles around---a baby had been born to an old woman! Plus, an angel had appeared to the baby's father, who had been unable to speak for nine months! Everyone who heard about it knew that Zechariah and Elizabeth had a special son for whom God had a special plan.

The people of Israel had been given many laws by God, one of which concerned baby boys. All of them were supposed to be circumcised on the eighth day of their lives. To be circumcised means to have a little piece of skin removed from a boy's private parts. It hurts for a little while, but quickly heals like any other cut. All the Israelite boys were supposed to be circumcised in order to mark them as being God's people. It showed that they belonged to God.

Like all other baby boys in Israel, John the Baptist was circumcised on the eighth day of his life, and that is when he was given the name *John* according to the instructions of the angel who appeared to his father. *John* means "God is very kind."

On the day of John's circumcision, his father was suddenly able to speak once again, and the first thing he spoke was praise to God. Soon after, the Holy Spirit spoke through him in a beautiful prophecy. If you listened to it closely, you probably noticed that the prophecy was more about Jesus than John. That's because Jesus was a million times more important than John. John was only a man made great by God. Jesus *was* God. Zechariah's prophecy revealed that it was God's plan for John to prepare the way for Jesus to begin His ministry.

What did Zechariah's prophecy say regarding Jesus? It revealed that Jesus was God. It said that *God* would *visit* His people (see Luke 1:68).

When He visited, God would redeem His people (see Luke 1:68). In the New Testament, the word *redeem* means to purchase someone's freedom from being a slave. Before we were born again, we were slaves to selfishness, sin and Satan.

Zechariah's prophecy also revealed that Jesus would be a mighty Savior (see Luke 1:69). We needed someone to save us from the penalty for our sins: eternal separation from God in hell. Through our Savior, our sins have been forgiven because of God's wonderful mercy (see Luke 1:77-78).

That Savior would be a descendant of King David, just as God had promised David a thousand years before (see Luke 1:69b-70).

Jesus would also save God's people from their enemies. Through Jesus, we've already been saved from our spiritual enemies: Satan and his evil spirits. They can't control us as they used to. Now, as Zechariah said, we can serve God without fear of them (see Luke 1:74). And one day, all of God's people will be saved from their physical enemies, when we live in God's eternal kingdom. There won't be anyone there who hates us.

The truth that Jesus would bring to the people of the earth would be like light coming down from heaven. No longer would we have to stumble around in darkness, not knowing where we are going. His truth would guide us into peace (see Luke 1:79). Aren't you glad that Jesus came?

Q. Is there any evidence in today's reading that Zechariah was not only temporarily mute, but also temporarily deaf?

A. Yes. Read Luke 1:62 closely. If Zechariah had been able to hear, his friends and relatives wouldn't have needed to communicate to him "by making gestures."

Q. If you were unable to speak for nine months, what would be the first words out of your mouth when your speech was restored? Why?

Application: *Isn't it amazing that God had a plan for John's life even before he was born? Did you know that, according to Ephesians 2:10, God also had a plan for our lives even before we were born? All of God's children are somewhat like John the Baptist. Like John, our main job is to get people ready to meet the Lord.*

NOTES:

Matthew Tells the Story of Jesus' Birth
Matthew 1:18-25

When two people are engaged, that means they've promised to marry each other but are not yet actually married until their wedding. In our day, engaged people sometimes get "disengaged," and when they do, it's usually because one of them has discovered something about the other person that wasn't known previously. (That's why it's a good idea to get to know a person as much as you can before promising to marry him or her.)

That was the situation for Mary and Joseph. When Joseph discovered that Mary was pregnant, he figured that she had fallen in love with someone else. That greatly alarmed him for several reasons. First, Mary undoubtedly told Joseph that she would marry him because she loved him. But the baby in her belly indicated that she loved another man, and so she had lied to him. No one wants to marry a liar.

Second, in order for Mary to become pregnant, she must have had a sexual relationship with that other man. That meant she had broken one of the Ten Commandments, and so she was also an adulteress (or more technically, a fornicator). No one wants to marry an adulteress.

Third, in her defense, Mary surely explained to Joseph that the baby in her belly was conceived by the Holy Spirit. If she did, Joseph obviously didn't believe her. He must have thought she was going crazy, claiming to have seen an angel who told her she would give birth to God's Son! No wonder Joseph decided to break their engagement! He was a wise man.

Joseph was also a very good man. Even though he was surely very hurt by what he discovered, he knew that everyone would think badly about Mary if they also knew what he did. So he decided to break his engagement quietly, so as not to embarrass her. The

Bible says that when we love someone, we won't want to advertise his or her sins, but keep quiet about them.

God, who knows everything, knew what Joseph was planning to do, so He had an angel appear to Joseph in a dream. The angel explained the truth about Mary's baby, and instructed him to name the child Jesus, which means "the Lord saves." Jesus would save us from our sins, and that was the main reason He came into the world. Joseph was greatly relieved to learn the truth, and he did what the angel told him.

Q. There were probably many people who passed judgment on Joseph and Mary when they saw that Mary was pregnant but not yet married to Joseph. It must have really hurt them. Have you ever had someone believe something bad about you that wasn't true? What should you do when that happens?

A. You should try to explain the truth to those who have passed judgment on you, hoping that they'll realize their error. But, even if they don't, you can be thankful that God knows the truth and trust that He will eventually clear you, just as He did Mary.

Q. Have you ever believed something bad about someone else that you later discovered wasn't true? Why did you believe it at first? What did you learn from that experience?

Q. Do you think you will ever get married? How long do you think you should be friends with a person before agreeing to get married? What are the most important traits you should look for in a person to marry?

A. Obedience to God and unselfishness.

Application: *We should always believe the best about people until we know differently, and when we do, if we love them, we will hide their sins, not tell everyone about them. NOTES:*

Luke Tells Us More About the Birth of Jesus
Luke 2:1-20

Through the Old Testament prophet Micah, God had foretold that the Messiah would be born in Bethlehem: "But you, O Bethlehem...are only a small village in Judah. Yet a ruler of Israel will come from you, one whose origins are from the distant past" (Micah 5:2). So it was no accident that Mary and Joseph were in Bethlehem when Jesus was born. Before the world was created, God knew that around the year 6 B.C. the leader of the Roman Empire would decree that a census be taken of all the people in his domain. For that reason, Joseph and Mary had to journey about 65 miles to register in the town of Joseph's ancestor, David.

When we think about Jesus being born, we often imagine a picture similar to what we've seen on the front of Christmas cards: a soft golden glow surrounding a beautiful mother with a baby in her arms, as her husband and the animals of the manger scene adoringly watch. But Jesus' birth was not such a pretty picture. First, giving birth to a baby is not an easy thing to do---just ask your mom about when you were born! Then ask her how she would have enjoyed delivering you in a stinky barn, right on the floor, after several days of traveling! That is probably how Jesus was born. Mary laid him in a manger, which is a nice word for an animal feeding trough. How would you like to sleep in a box where animals had eaten and slobbered? Jesus went through a lot of trouble to become a human being, and that shows us how much He loves us.

I wonder if Mary and Joseph complained to each other about all their troubles. Just to register their names in Bethlehem, they had to make a long journey when Mary was very pregnant, and Mary had to give birth in very unpleasant surroundings. They probably didn't realize that they were right in the center of God's will, fulfilling an ancient prophecy. We often grumble about circumstances in our lives when we don't see God's plan. But if we could see our circumstances through God's eyes, we would rejoice. And so we should!

God's perspective of Mary and Joseph's plight was revealed to the shepherds of today's reading. The multitudes of angels that God allowed them to see were praising God because the Son of God, the long-awaited Messiah, the Savior, had been born! At that time, it was the greatest event of history! Those angels had been sent from heaven to tell them the wonderful news because God was so excited about the birth of His Son. Just like when you were born, your dad wanted everyone to know about it!

Q. Why are we certain that the prophet Micah, in his prophecy about a ruler coming from Bethlehem, was talking about Jesus, and not some other ruler of Israel?

A. We are certain because Micah identified that ruler as being someone "whose origins are from the distant past" (see Micah 5:2). The Jewish leaders in Jesus' time knew that Micah could have only been speaking of the Messiah, even if they didn't understand that the Messiah would be God Himself, who existed from eternity (see Matt. 2:3-6).

Q. Looking back at your life, do you think that anything has happened to you that you complained about at the time, but that God was excited about because He could see the whole picture? Could that be true of anything you are complaining about right now in your life?

Application: *The Bible says, "God causes everything to work together for the good of those who love God and are called according to His purpose for them" (Romans 8:28). God doesn't cause all things, and not all things are good, but God does cause all things to work together for good. Since that's true, we should maintain a good attitude, even when things don't go the way we want them to.*

NOTES:

The Records of Jesus' Ancestors
Matt 1:1-17 Luke 3:23-38

What long lists these are! Aren't you glad you don't have to memorize all those names for your history class?

Why are these two lists of Jesus' ancestors not identical? Probably because Matthew recorded Jesus' ancestry through His stepfather, Joseph, and Luke recorded Jesus' ancestry through His mother, Mary. Also, Matthew's list goes back to Abraham, whereas Luke's list goes all the way back to Adam. If you'll compare the lists closely, you'll discover that both Mary and Joseph were descendants of King David, but through two different sons. On both lists, the people from Abraham to David are the same, except that Matthew left out one name, perhaps to make his list easier to remember as three segments of fourteen generations, as he mentioned (see Matthew 1:17).

Did you know that some of the people on Luke's list are your ancestors? The reason is because they're everyone's ancestors! All of us are descendants of Adam, Seth, Enosh, Kenan, Mahalalel, Jared, Enoch, Methuselah, Lamech and Noah, so all of them are your great, great, great, great (and so on) grandfathers! You'll get to meet at least some of them in heaven someday!

To the Jewish people, keeping track of their ancestry was very important. All of them were descendants of Abraham, Isaac and Jacob. Jacob was renamed *Israel* by God, and that is why all his descendants are called "the people of Israel" or "the Israelites." Jacob had twelve sons who became twelve tribes, and all their descendants knew from what tribe they came.

There are two main reasons why these two lists are so important to us. First, because they prove that Jesus was a real person of history. Some people foolishly think that the story of Jesus is just a myth or fairy tale (like Santa Claus) that someone made up. But Jesus was a person who really was born just like everyone else. He was a person of history just as much as George Washington or Abraham Lincoln.

Second, these lists are important because God had promised in the Old Testament that the Messiah would be a descendant of Abraham, Isaac, Jacob, Judah, Jesse and David. If Jesus had not been a descendant of those men, we could be sure that He was not really the Messiah. Matthew and Luke's lists prove, however, that Jesus was in the lineage of all six of those men through both His mother and stepfather.

Q. Luke recorded 76 generations from Adam until Jesus. If each generation was twenty-five years apart, how long ago could we conclude that Adam was created?

A. About 3,900 years [(25 x 76) + 2000]. If we use a high estimate for the average rate of growth of the world's population over the past centuries (.5%) and work backward from that, we can conclude that the earth's population consisted of just a few people around 4,000 years before Jesus, about the time of Noah's flood.

Q. Then why do some scientists say that the fossilized human bones they discover are millions of years old?

A. Because the dating methods of those scientists are very questionable. They try to determine the age of the bones based upon their location in the layers of rock, and the dates of those layers of rocks is a guess. Many scientists assume the rock layers were laid down gradually, over billions of years, underneath ancient oceans. They don't consider the fact of a worldwide flood during Noah's time, when rock layers could have formed very quickly. Nor do they seem to consider the fact that dead bodies don't normally turn into fossilized bones. The average dead dinosaur didn't fossilize---it rotted away. Only under catastrophic circumstances do living things fossilize, which is what may have happened during the worldwide flood of the Bible. People and animals may have been buried quickly under tons of sediment that is now exposed thousands of years later through the process of erosion.

Q. From which tribe of Israel was Jesus descended?

A. Judah

Application: *Since Jesus was a real person of history who was also the Son of God, we should want to learn all we can about Him and do what He says.*

NOTES:

Baby Jesus Presented in the Temple
Luke 2:21-40

When Jesus was just a newborn, He was like any other baby. He couldn't walk or talk, He cried when He wanted to be fed, and He dirtied His diapers regularly. Isn't it funny to think that God dirtied His diapers? More than making us chuckle, however, it should make us realize how much God must love us---He humbled Himself that much in order to save us from our sins.

In the Law that God gave to the descendants of Israel, there were several rules relating to the birth of children. Those rules revealed that God wanted His people never to forget how special it was to have a baby. All babies are made in God's image and are His own potential children, and parents should never forget that. Becoming a parent is a very serious and important thing. God required Israelite parents to bring their first-born sons to the Temple in Jerusalem to present them before Him there. Perhaps one reason for this law was to help new parents understand how valuable their children were and how important their responsibility was in His eyes. It was a way of saying to God, "This is not as much *my* child as it is *Your* child. Therefore, I will raise this child as You want me to."

Mothers were also required to offer a sacrifice at the Temple several weeks after their babies were born (see Lev. 12:1-8). This was a way of expressing thanks to God for giving them their babies, and it also served as a reminder to them of how good God had been to them in spite of their sins. They shouldn't think that having a baby was a sign of God's approval of their lives. Sometimes people think that God's blessings are proof that they are holy and fully pleasing to God, but it often only means that God is merciful and good. He is good to everyone, even to bad people! Anyone who has a baby should be thankful for God's goodness.

Simeon must have been a very spiritual man who studied the Scriptures closely. He knew God would keep His many promises to send the Savior, and must have hoped and prayed that he would live to see that day. God revealed to him that he would not die until his desire was realized. The Holy Spirit led him to baby Jesus the day that Mary and Joseph brought Him to the Temple. Simeon also knew that because God had sent His Son into the world, every human being would be faced with a decision: Would they reject or receive Him? Jesus' coming into the world would reveal what was in people's hearts. Because of the hardness of their hearts, many people of Israel would reject Jesus, and it would be "their undoing" just as Simeon predicted. That means they would go to hell. But to those who receive Jesus, it is their "greatest joy," because they know their sins are forgiven and they are going to heaven one day.

The Bible doesn't tell us much about the childhood of Jesus. We did learn today that He grew up in the town of Nazareth. We also read that He was "filled with wisdom beyond his years" (Luke 2:40), so He wasn't like a normal child in that respect. We'll learn in two days that when He was twelve years old, He had more spiritual wisdom than your parents probably do right now!

Q. What do you think Simeon meant when he told Mary that a "sword would pierce [her] very soul"?

A. She would be convicted by what Jesus would say and have to make a decision to obey or disobey Him.

Q. What do you think it means to have Jesus be your "greatest joy"?

A. It means that Jesus is the most special person in your life. Your relationship with Him is the most valuable thing you possess. Thinking about Him and what He has done for you should make you very happy on the inside.

Q. Has Jesus become your "greatest joy" yet?

Application: *Jesus was the most special person ever to have lived because He was the Son of God. Therefore, He should be more important than anything in our lives, and it should show by how we live our lives.*

NOTES:

The Wise Men Visit Jesus
Matthew 2:1-23

Mary and Joseph remained in Bethlehem for at least a few weeks after Jesus was born, and it may well have been during that time when the wise men visited Him. They had seen a star appear in the sky about two years earlier that led them to Jerusalem. Unfortunately, we don't know much about those wise men. We can assume that the new star they saw was placed in the sky by God, and that He somehow revealed the significance of the star to them. We don't know, however, which country they came from or how long they traveled. If they departed from their home country soon after they first saw the star, they started on their journey almost two years before Jesus was born! It's quite obvious that they knew Jesus was worth traveling a long way to see, and that He was worthy to be worshipped and given expensive gifts appropriate for kings. He was God!

Wicked King Herod didn't like hearing the news that a baby had been born who was destined to be king of the Jews, because at that time, he was a king over the Jewish people. (Herod hadn't been elected by the Jewish people to be king, but was appointed to be king by the Roman government that then controlled Israel.) Herod wanted to kill the new baby, but all he knew about the child was that He had been born in Bethlehem (as the prophet Micah had predicted), and that His special star had appeared in the sky about two years before. So Herod told the wise men that once they found the child, they should return and tell him so that he could go to Bethlehem and worship Him also. He was lying of course, and was really planning to kill Jesus. Herod was so evil that when he realized that the wise men weren't going to return to him with the details he requested, he ordered that every boy two years old and younger in the region of Bethlehem be killed by Roman soldiers. It was just as horrible as you can imagine, and Jeremiah had predicted it about 600 years earlier in a prophecy about Rachel, the wife of Israel, weeping for her dead children. The murdered boys were perhaps some of Rachel's descendants through her sons Joseph and Benjamin. Rachel herself had died in Bethlehem.

We are blessed to live in a nation where no one has the kind of absolute power that Herod had. No one in the United States has the authority to order the mass killing of people he doesn't like. But no matter where injustice exists, we know that God will ultimately bring justice because He is loving and fair. Did you notice that it wasn't long after the slaughter of the little boys in Bethlehem that Herod died? (see Matthew 2:19). People always "reap what they sow," which means that God will treat them like they treat others. Unless Herod repented of his horrible sins and believed in Jesus, when he died he went to hell and has been suffering there ever since.

Q. The wise men from the east brought Jesus some very expensive gifts, including gold. Can you think of a reason why Jesus may have needed those expensive things?

A. It's possible that Mary and Joseph used those gifts to support their little family during their flight to Egypt. If that was the case, God used the wise men to provide for their needs until they could return to Nazareth. There Joseph could support his family as a carpenter.

Q. What makes murder wrong?

A. Murder is wrong for several reasons. First, because every human being is created in God's image, and when a person is murdered, it is the killing of one who looks something like God. When someone angrily destroys or defaces a photograph of another person, it is an offence against the person in the photograph. If for no other reason, we should respect other human beings because they're created in God's image. Second, murder is wrong because every person is loved by God, so no one has the right to take the life of another person. When someone commits a murder, he has taken the life of someone who was loved by God. Murder is the highest form of selfishness.

Application: *Wise people know that Jesus is worth traveling to see, even if it takes months. He deserves to receive their best gifts, and is worthy to be worshiped. We are a wise family!*

NOTES:

Jesus as a Young Boy
Luke 2:41-52

One of the many laws that the Israelites were required to obey was to observe the yearly Passover festival in Jerusalem. It was a time to remember when God delivered the Israelites from slavery in Egypt over a thousand years before Jesus was born. God's destroying angel had killed all the firstborn Egyptians, but he didn't harm the firstborn Israelites because they had obeyed God's instructions to kill a lamb and mark their doors with its blood. When the destroying angel came to a house that was marked with the blood, he "passed over" it. The Egyptians were so afraid of the Israelites' God that they released them from slavery, and all the people of Israel left Egypt to journey to a new land God would give them.

God had said that from then on, the Israelites should kill a lamb every year on that same day to remind them of what He had done for them in Egypt. He also wanted them to understand that their sins could be forgiven only through a sacrifice that served as a substitute. Of course, an animal can't really serve as a substitute for a human being, so we know that the animal sacrifices only served to reveal what Jesus would do for us when He died as our substitute on the cross. That is why Jesus is referred to as "the Lamb of God" in the Bible. Jesus died on the cross during a Passover festival.

When Jesus was young, He journeyed every year to Jerusalem to celebrate the Passover with Mary, Joseph and many other people who lived in Nazareth. The festival lasted for one week, and then everyone returned to their home towns. Mary and Joseph, probably knowing that Jesus was responsible enough to take care of Himself, didn't worry that He wasn't with them when they departed from Jerusalem. They assumed He was with their friends and relatives traveling back to Nazareth with them. Once they discovered He was missing, however, they went back to Jerusalem and frantically searched for Him, finally finding Him three days later talking to the religious leaders in the Temple. Mary and Joseph were probably very angry with Jesus at first, but they could hardly remain angry since He was amazing everyone in the Temple with His deep understanding of spiritual matters. (If you were missing for three days, your parents would be very angry with you, but if they found you at school teaching your teachers and the principal, they would probably cool down quickly!)

Jesus was surprised that Mary and Joseph had searched for a whole day in Jerusalem before they found Him. He thought they should have known right where He'd be, in His "Father's house," the Temple. But Mary and Joseph didn't understand what He meant, which is often the case with parents and their children!

Q. At twelve years of age, Jesus was most interested in spiritual matters. Does that mean He was a nerd?

A. No, it means that He was a very wise boy with whom God was pleased. Kids are often very interested in sports, hobbies and other fun activities, and there is nothing wrong with those interests. However, wise young people are most interested in learning more about their relationship with God. Knowing and obeying God should be the most important thing in everyone's life, young and old.

Q. Because Jesus remained in Jerusalem when His parents left for Nazareth, does that mean He was disobedient to His parents?

A. Although it may seem that way, it couldn't be that way because disobedience to parents is a sin, and Jesus never sinned. Mary and Joseph apparently departed from Jerusalem without being certain Jesus was with them, assuming that He was with others who were also departing. It could be considered a case of negligence on their part. Perhaps when Jesus discovered that His parents had departed without Him, He assumed they would soon return upon discovery of His absence. And the best place to wait for them was at the Temple, as that would surely be the first place they would look for

Him, knowing who He was. One other possibility is that Jesus' heavenly Father had instructed Him to remain at the Temple. If that was the case, Jesus had to obey regardless of how Mary and Joseph reacted. The only time it is acceptable to disobey parents is when obeying them would mean disobeying God.

Application: *Since we are followers of Jesus, we should obey our parents just as Jesus obeyed Mary and Joseph.*

NOTES:

DAY 14

John the Baptist Prepares the Way for Jesus
Luke 3:1-20

John the Baptist was the greatest evangelist who has ever lived, and today the world needs more evangelists who will imitate him. An evangelist's job is to preach the gospel, and that is what John did. He told people that the Messiah whom they had been waiting for was about to appear. They should get ready for Him by repenting, which means to stop doing what they knew was wrong and start doing what they knew was right.

John was called by God to do his job, and he was specially anointed by the Holy Spirit to preach powerfully. John told the people the truth, and he didn't water it down. First, he told them not to trust that they were saved just because they were descendants of Abraham. Sometimes people think that they are saved because their parents are saved, but God has no grandchildren, just children!

Second, John warned the people that they were sinners who were in danger of suffering God's judgment. If they didn't repent, they would burn in the fires of hell for eternity. That is the truth, and truthful evangelists will warn people about hell.

Third, John told them that if they truly believed and repented, their lives would show it. People who didn't change weren't really saved. People who keep on sinning just as they did before their so-called conversion won't get into heaven.

John used examples that the people he was preaching to could understand. Most of the people were farmers, so John compared Jesus to a farmer separating the chaff from the grain. The farmers in John's day used a tool that looked like a big fork, which they would shove into a pile of wheat cuttings and then throw them up into the air. The wind would blow the chaff away (the part that couldn't be eaten), and the heavier grain would fall into one pile below. John said that Jesus would be doing the same thing, only with people instead of grain. He would separate believers from nonbelievers, and just like the farmer who burns up the chaff, Jesus would cast the unbelievers into hell. The believers, however, Jesus would gather into His "barn," bringing them into heaven. Everybody is in one of only two categories: grain or chaff, believers or nonbelievers, hell-bound or heaven-bound.

John didn't preach using only general terms that people could interpret any way they liked. He told people specifically what they should do. If they were sincere about repenting, they would quit acting selfishly and start considering others, treating them just like they wanted to be treated. John told the people to share their belongings and food with the poor, to do their work honestly and to be content with their wages.

John was also a very humble man. Although God used him in a mighty way, and Jesus later stated that he was the greatest man who ever lived, John considered himself unworthy to be even a slave of Jesus. He knew that Jesus was a million times more important than he, and it was his job to point people to Jesus. If only every evangelist today was like John!

Many people who heard John preach were convicted of their sins, and John told them that they should be baptized in the Jordan River as a public testimony of their repentance. When someone believes in Jesus, he should be baptized as soon as possible, and he should do it in front of other people. Jesus commanded those who believe in Him to be baptized (see Matthew 28:19), and so when someone who claims to be a believer in Jesus refuses to be baptized in obedience to what Jesus commanded, we know he really doesn't believe that Jesus is the Son of God. When new Christians are baptized, they are making a public declaration that they have become followers of Jesus and that they are turning away from sin. Have you been baptized yet? If you are a believer in Jesus, you should be baptized as soon as you can.

Q. We read today that Herod had John the Baptist put in prison. Could that Herod have been the same Herod who ordered the killing of the baby boys in Bethlehem?

A. No, he died when Jesus was very young. This Herod was one of his sons, and he was evil like his father.

Q. Have you become a follower of Jesus yet? Becoming a follower of Jesus begins with repentance, and if you have never yet repented of sin, you haven't begun following Jesus. If you have already become a follower of Jesus, what changes were evident in your life after you repented?

Application: *As followers of Jesus, we should be living lives that are different than those who are not saved. The things we say and do should make us stand out from people who are not followers of Jesus.*

NOTES:

Jesus is Baptized by John the Baptist
Matt 3:13-17; John 1:29-34

John had baptized many people who had repented and believed his message that the Messiah would soon appear. When Jesus came to be baptized, John didn't yet realize that He was the Messiah, so it wasn't for that reason that he was hesitant to baptize Jesus. He must have been hesitant because, when he compared himself to perfect and sinless Jesus, his own sinfulness was evident. That is why John suggested that Jesus baptize him! This reveals to us that Jesus had a reputation of being a very holy person, which we would have expected anyway since we know Jesus never sinned.

It was right after John baptized Jesus that John saw the Holy Spirit descend upon Him in the form of a dove. God had foretold John that when he saw that happen, it would reveal the person who was the Savior. Can you imagine how John felt at that moment when Jesus came up out of the water? His own relative, the most holy person he had ever met, was actually God's Son! For thirty years Jesus had kept it a secret! From then on John began to tell everyone that Jesus was the Son of God. The secret was out!

John also understood something about the main reason why Jesus became a man, because he began referring to Jesus as "the Lamb of God who takes away the sin of the world" (John 1:29). For thousands of years the people of Israel had sacrificed lambs during every Passover, just as God had commanded. But those lambs only served to prefigure Jesus, who would die for everyone's sins, not just covering them, but, as John said, taking them away. If you are a believer in Jesus, you should know that He has taken away your sins. In God's eyes, you aren't just a sinner who was found guilty and then forgiven, you are a new person who has been declared "not guilty"! Wow!

Q. Why didn't John call Jesus "Lord" when he objected to baptizing Him?

A. Because John didn't know at that point that Jesus was Lord.

Q. Why do you think Jesus wanted to be baptized by John like everyone else?

A. It couldn't have been because Jesus needed to repent like everyone else, because He was sinless. Jesus told John that He should be baptized in order to "do everything that is right" (Matthew 3:15). Some people (including myself) think that Jesus was baptized as a way of foreshadowing His death on the cross. Picture it this way: Thousands of sinful people being baptized in the Jordan River, washing their dirty sins into the water, and then Jesus, who was clean and sinless, going down into the water and coming up with everyone's sins on Him. That is what happened on the cross, when Jesus took the sins of the world on Himself and suffered as our substitute.

Application: *Once we realize and believe, just as John the Baptist did, that Jesus is the Son of God, we need to tell other people, especially those who are searching for the truth.*

NOTES:

DAY 16
Satan Tempts Jesus
Luke 4:1-13

In order for Jesus to die on the cross bearing our sins, it was necessary that He have no sins of His own. If He had committed any sins, then He couldn't have taken our sins and died as our substitute. Therefore, Jesus had to be sinless, and in order to be proven sinless, He had to be faced with temptation (it's easy not to sin when there's no temptation). That is why the Holy Spirit led Jesus out into the desert to be tempted by the devil.

Jesus' temptations in the desert, however, were not the only times Satan tempted Him, because the Bible tells us that Jesus "faced all of the same temptations we do, yet he did not sin" (Hebrews 4:15). Jesus was tempted to do wrong throughout His entire life. He was tempted to lie, cheat, steal, disobey His parents and act selfishly, but He never gave in to those temptations even once.

We read today that Satan twice tried to get Jesus to doubt what God the Father had told Him just a few days before: that He was the Son of God. Satan always tries to make people doubt what God has said. That is how he got Adam and Eve to disobey the Lord. Anytime we hear something that does not agree with what God's Word says, we should realize that it is a lie from Satan. Satan can only fool people who don't know or don't believe what God has said. But once you know and believe the truth, you can't be tricked into believing one of Satan's lies. People who know and believe what God has said don't have to be scared of Satan. He can't hurt them at all.

Knowing that Jesus was hungry after fasting for forty days, Satan tempted Him to change a stone into a loaf of bread so He would have something to eat. But Jesus responded by quoting what God had said, "People need more than bread for their life" (Luke 4:4). When the devil tempts us, we overcome him by knowing, believing, saying and obeying what God has said.

According to the Bible, Satan is "the god of this evil world" (2 Corinthians 4:4). That means he is controlling all the people in the world who are not submitted to Jesus, and also controlling all the evil spirits who rule over those unsaved people. Since most people are unsaved, Satan has power over the majority of people in the world in practically every country. God has allowed him to rule over that domain, called in the Bible, "the kingdom of darkness." Satan offered Jesus the second-in-command position over his worldwide kingdom if Jesus would join his side, proving His allegiance by bowing down before the devil and worshiping him. Again, Jesus responded by knowing, believing, saying and obeying what God had said: "You must worship the Lord your God; serve him only." Jesus knew that one day He would be ruling over the entire earth and that Satan would one day be banished to hell forever.

Finally, Satan tried to twist some Bible verses to make them mean something that they really didn't say. He quoted from Psalm 91, saying that it promised Jesus protection if He jumped from the highest point of the Temple. But Jesus knew what the rest of the Old Testament had to say, and He knew that it would be wrong and foolish to jump off a high place and expect God to protect Him. That would be testing God. Again Jesus overcame the devil by knowing, believing, saying and obeying God's Word.

Aren't you glad Jesus didn't give in to any of Satan's temptations? If He had, you and I couldn't have been saved!

Q. What temptations have you faced in the last week? Did you give in or resist? What can you do the next time you face the same temptation?

Q. When you are tempted, does that mean that the devil himself is in your presence, right beside you, suggesting that you do the wrong thing?

A. No, the devil can only be in one place at one time. One of Satan's evil spirits might be present who is tempting you.

However, the Bible says that temptation comes "from the lure of our evil desires" (James 1:14). That means we can be tempted without the help of Satan or one of his evil spirits.

Application: *When we face a temptation to do wrong, we should think of what God has said to do. If we don't know, we should find out what God has said to do. Then we should do it.*

NOTES:

Jesus' First Disciples
John 1:35-51

John the Baptist had a group of disciples with whom he was very close. They were men who were very excited that the Messiah was about to appear, and John shared with them everything he knew about spiritual things. Together, they were anticipating that they would soon meet the Savior of the world.

When John saw the Holy Spirit come upon Jesus, he knew that Jesus was the one they'd been waiting for, and he undoubtedly told his disciples soon after. Jesus, however, departed for the desert immediately after He was baptized, where He spent forty days. Thus John never had the opportunity to point at Jesus and tell anyone who He was. After the forty days, Jesus returned to a place where John was baptizing, and John began pointing Him out as "the Lamb of God." Two of John's disciples were the very first people who learned this wonderful news. One of those two was Andrew, and the other is unnamed in today's reading, but many people think he may have been John, who became one of Jesus' twelve disciples and who wrote the Gospel of John.

When people find out that Jesus is the Son of God, they naturally want their friends and families to know also, and so Andrew went and told his brother, Simon. Then he brought Simon to Jesus, and amazingly, Jesus already knew his name! Jesus also told him that one day people would call him a different name, Peter, which means "rock." Jesus knew the Holy Spirit would change Simon into a man who would be firm in his faith and hard to move, like a rock. God would use him in a mighty way to lay the foundation of the early church.

When Philip brought his friend Nathanael to meet Jesus, Nathanael was surprised that Jesus also knew some things about him. Jesus knew he was a very honest man, and He apparently had a vision of Nathanael sitting under a fig tree where Philip found him. Because of this, Nathanael was immediately convinced that Jesus was the Son of God. Jesus promised him that he would one day be in heaven and see angels. That's something to which everyone who believes that Jesus is the Son of God can look forward!

Q. As we learned from reading about Peter and Nathanael, God knows everything about you, including your personality, your past, present and future. How should that affect your relationship with Him?

A. It should motivate you to obey Him, trust Him, and want to get to know Him better. It should encourage you to seek His direction for your life.

Q. All the men we read about today, except Nathanael, became members of Jesus' band of twelve disciples. Many people think that Nathanael was also called Bartholomew, and if he was, then he, too, became one of the twelve. Can you think of any reason why Jesus may have chosen those men rather than others?

A. One obvious reason Jesus chose them was because they were very interested in Him. God chooses and uses spiritually hungry people.

Application: *Like Peter, the more we get to know Jesus, the more we'll be changed to become like Jesus. We can trust that Jesus is going to complete the good work He's begun in us.*

NOTES:

Four Fishermen Become Fishers of Men
Luke 5:1-11

As we learned before, Andrew and his brother Peter had already met Jesus through John the Baptist. Both Andrew and Peter were from the Galilean village of Bethsaida, and worked together as fishermen on the Sea of Galilee with their friends, James and John, who were also brothers.

One day shortly after Peter and Andrew had met Jesus, Jesus was preaching to great crowds of people along the shore of the Sea of Galilee. They were probably sitting on the steep banks as Jesus preached by the water's edge. But there were so many people who wanted to hear what He was saying that the crowd kept pressing in to get closer. Jesus didn't have a sound system to amplify His voice, so if people wanted to hear Him, they had to get close. As a result, they were forcing Jesus out into the water! So Jesus stepped into Peter's boat and asked him to push it out a little way from shore so He could continue teaching while sitting in the boat.

When we give or lend something to Jesus, He always pays us back, and so He did for Peter after borrowing his boat. Peter and his partners had worked hard all night but hadn't caught a single fish. (The reason they had fished at night was because that was the best time to catch fish. Perhaps they used a lantern to attract the fish at night to their nets.) Even though Peter had already cleaned his nets and was probably ready to head home to get some sleep, Jesus instructed him to put down his nets in the deep water during the daylight, promising him that he would catch a lot of fish. It certainly didn't seem like a very good idea to an intelligent fisherman. It sounded like it would be a waste of time, but Peter had already witnessed the fact that Jesus knew things supernaturally, and so he did what Jesus said.

Amazingly, Peter's net was soon so full of fish that it began to tear. So Peter yelled to James and John on the shore to bring their boat out, and when they did, they filled both boats with so many fish that they were close to sinking! Imagine how funny it must have been to watch them try to row their heavy boats successfully to shore without sinking or losing any fish!

It was a *huge* catch of fish, more than anyone had ever caught before, and Peter and his partners knew it was miraculous. They were stunned when they looked at the big piles of fish in their boats. Peter, realizing how much money all those fish were worth at the market, couldn't believe how good God had been to him. He knew he didn't deserve such a blessing, and so he fell at Jesus' feet, confessing his sinfulness. But Jesus told him not to be afraid, and told him he would soon have a new job: catching people instead of fish!

Q. When Peter realized how kind God had been to him, even when he didn't deserve it, he became a changed man. He was saved. What evidence is there in what we just read that indicates Peter repented and believed in Jesus?

A. First, Peter humbled himself by falling at Jesus' feet. Not many people, especially grown men, and especially tough fishermen, would fall at someone's feet unless they truly believed that person was very special. Second, Peter called Jesus *Lord* . That indicates Peter believed Jesus was worthy to control his life. Third, Peter admitted that he was a sinner. Before anyone can be saved, they must admit that they are guilty sinners who need a Savior. And fourth, Peter began following Jesus from that day on, leaving everything behind. He made obeying Jesus the most important thing in his life.

Q. How was it, do you suppose, that Peter, Andrew, James and John were able just to quit their jobs to follow Jesus? How did they have money to live?

A. If they sold the great quantity of fish that Jesus just blessed them with, that probably provided their needs for quite some time. There's a proverb that says, "Where God guides, God provides." Also, many people supported the ministry of Jesus by giving Him money, so Jesus was able to take care of all His disciples. Finally, it is quite probable that some of the four fishermen we read about today were not yet married, so they didn't have families to support.

Q. Can you find any evidence in today's reading that Jesus was in the boat with Peter when they caught all the fish?

A. We read that Peter fell at Jesus' feet when he realized what had happened (see Luke 5:8-9). If Peter was in the boat (which he apparently was), then Jesus must have been there also. Additionally, Jesus told Peter that he would be catching men before the boats landed (see Luke 5:10-11).

Application: *It is always smart to do what Jesus said and trust His promises, even when others might think we are foolish. Jesus can't lie, and He knows what He's talking about!*

NOTES:

Jesus Changes Water into Wine
John 2:1-11

If you've ever been to a wedding reception, you probably remember having lots of food to eat and wedding punch to drink. Can you imagine how embarrassed the bride and bridegroom would be if people were standing in line to get punch and were told the punch had run out? The wedding guests would know that the hosts hadn't planned properly, and in a hot climate like Israel, their thirst would certainly aggravate the situation. This is what occurred at this wedding in the village of Cana that Jesus, His mother and disciples attended.

When Mary told Jesus about the wine running out, Jesus responded with words we wouldn't have expected. "How does that concern you and me?" Jesus asked. "My time has not yet come" (John 2:4). If we read through the whole Gospel of John, we discover that Jesus spoke often about His "time" coming, and it becomes obvious that He was always referring to the time when He would die for the sins of the world. So when Jesus responded to Mary's statement about the lack of wine, He must have been thinking about people lacking, not wine, but something that wouldn't be provided until He died. It's possible that Jesus was referring to His own blood, which was symbolized by wine at the Last Supper. Or He may have been speaking about the Holy Spirit, who is sometimes symbolized by wine in the New Testament. Everyone needs to have his sins forgiven through the shedding of Jesus' blood and be born again by the Holy Spirit. Both of those are much greater needs than wine running out at a wedding feast. Jesus was concerned about *much* more important things than Mary was.

Jesus, however, must have been somewhat concerned about the lack of wine at the wedding feast because He performed a miracle to solve the problem. That miracle may also have had a deeper spiritual meaning, because Jesus didn't change just *any* water into wine---He changed water that was used by the Jews for the purpose of purification rites into wine. Because of the many laws that God gave the Jews to keep, they were very conscious (or aware) of their sinfulness, and they were always trying to keep themselves symbolically purified by various washings with water. But since Jesus died for us, cleansing us from all the guilt of our sins, we don't need any other way of getting spiritually clean. Knowing that we're cleansed, we can now enjoy ourselves, drinking Jesus' good wine. Now we can really celebrate!

But isn't it wrong to drink anything that is alcoholic? If so, why did Jesus change water into wine that day?

Historians tell us that the Jews always diluted their wine with water, so the amount of alcohol in their wine was very small. It was more like what we today call "grape juice" than what we today call wine. We must also remember that, other than water, wine was practically the only beverage people could drink back in Jesus' day, and the water that was available was often contaminated and undrinkable in the villages and cities. We have many choices of beverages today, so no one *has* to drink wine. Christians don't all agree if it is wrong for them to drink alcoholic beverages, but one thing all true Christians agree on is this: the Bible very clearly says that it is a sin to get drunk. Getting drunk starts with one drink, and if that one drink begins to cloud a person's thinking, he might more easily yield to the temptation for another drink and then another. The safest thing to do is completely abstain from all alcoholic drinks.

Alcohol has caused a lot of heartaches to multitudes of people. Many babies have been born with deformities because their mothers drank alcohol when they were pregnant. Many innocent people have been killed by drunk drivers. Many families have been ruined by parents who became addicted to alcohol. Because alcohol is responsible for so much that is evil and sinful, my advice to Christians is to abstain from drinking it at all. John certainly didn't record this miracle of Jesus changing water into watered-down wine for the purpose of encouraging Christians to drink modern alcoholic beverages. He recorded this miracle to prove that Jesus was the Son of God and to remind us of the wonderful salvation He's provided for us!

Q. Did you notice that the wine Jesus made was described by the master of ceremonies as being better than the first wine that ran out? Does this teach us anything about God?

A. Perhaps it does. It shows us that when God does something, He does a quality job, and He wants us to enjoy the best He has to offer us. He has provided a wonderful salvation for us that includes loads of benefits for all eternity, not just a temporary fixer-upper salvation that puts a band-aid on our problem. He doesn't want us to have mediocre families, but quality families, with truly loving relationships. Are you enjoying all the benefits of what God has to offer us?

Q. Does this miracle of Jesus' changing water into wine teach us anything about God's power?

A. Yes, it shows us that God can change anything into something else. If you believe in Jesus, He has changed you from a child of Satan into His own child. One day God will change your physical body into a brand new body that glows with His glory.

Application: *Because of this first miracle, Jesus' disciples believed in Him. For us, this miracle is one more proof that Jesus truly is the Son of God, and because we believe He is, we should trust and obey Him.*

NOTES:

DAY 20

The First Time Jesus Cleans Out the Temple
John 2:13-25

Many people like to hear about God's love, but they aren't interested in hearing about God's anger with sin and wrongdoing. Today's reading reveals that side of God. Jesus was obviously very angry about what was taking place in the Temple, and He reacted furiously.

What was Jesus so mad about? Of course, there's nothing sinful about buying or selling animals or exchanging money. Jesus was angry over the fact that the Temple in Jerusalem, a sacred place where His Father was supposed to be honored and worshipped, had been turned into a marketplace. The Temple was the place where the priests offered sacrifices to the Lord, and in the innermost part of the Temple, called "The Holy of Holies," God's presence resided. But in Jesus' day, the people around the Temple weren't focused on God or serving the people who came to worship God, but on making money. Not only that, but they were taking advantage of people who came from far away places to worship at the Temple, charging them very high prices to purchase animals and exchange their foreign currency. In another Gospel, the writer records Jesus saying to the merchants at the Temple, "'My Temple will be called a place of prayer,' *but you have turned it into a den of thieves"* (Matthew 21:13, emphasis added). There was dishonesty in their dealings, and God doesn't like that, as Jesus so clearly revealed.

What we've read today contains a lot of proof that Jesus was the Messiah and was God in the form of a human being. First, we learned that a verse in the Old Testament book of Psalms foretold that the Messiah would have very strong emotions about God's house, or Temple. That same Psalm also predicted that the Messiah would be given sour wine to quench His thirst, just as Jesus was when He hung on the cross (see Psalm 69:21 and Matthew 27:34, 48).

Second, if Jesus wasn't God, then He had no right to chase out the oxen and sheep or overturn the tables of the moneychangers, spilling their money all over the ground. Any person who was not God and who did such a thing would be guilty of not showing respect for the private property of other people. God created everything and owns everything, so *everyone* and his property belongs to Him! He can do what He wants with anyone's property, and Jesus, being God, knew He had that right.

Some of the Jewish leaders thought Jesus had no right to do what He did, and they asked Him to justify His actions. He responded by telling them about His resurrection, although they didn't understand what He was talking about. This is a third proof to us that Jesus was God. Not only did He come back to life after being dead for three days, He predicted it would happen three years before it did!

Q. Jesus told the Jewish leaders who questioned Him, "Destroy this temple, and in three days I will raise it up" (John 2:19). He was speaking of the temple of His body, but His listeners thought He was speaking about the Jerusalem Temple building. How was Jesus' body even more of God's temple than the Jerusalem Temple?

A. Because Jesus was actually God in the form of a human being, His body was much more a temple of God than the Temple building, which only contained God's presence in the innermost parts.

Q. In the final verses of today's reading, we read that Jesus didn't trust everyone who said they believed in Him. Why didn't He?

A. Because Jesus knew that people are often liars, and just because someone says he believes in Jesus doesn't prove he actually does. A person's actions speak louder than his words, and so the true proof that someone believes in Jesus is his obedience to the Lord.

Application: *Because Jesus has come into our temples, and because we are now temples of God, we should keep our temple clean from sin and anything that is not pleasing to Jesus.*

NOTES:

DAY 21

A Jewish Teacher Visits Jesus at Night
John 3:1-16

The Pharisees of Jesus' time were a very strict sect of Jews. They tried to follow all of God's laws fully as well as many laws they made up themselves, thinking they could earn their way to heaven. Nicodemus was not only a Pharisee, but also a member of the Jewish ruling council and a very well-known religious teacher. He was amazed by the miracles Jesus performed, and was convinced that Jesus was sent from God. However, he didn't yet know that Jesus was actually the divine Son of God. So Jesus knew He needed to explain some very important things to Nicodemus.

He began by telling Nicodemus that, in order to get into heaven, he had to be born a second time. Nicodemus didn't understand what Jesus meant. He couldn't imagine how he could ever go back inside his mother and be born another time! So Jesus explained that He wasn't talking about his *body* being born again through his mother, but his *spirit* being reborn through the Holy Spirit. The Bible says that every person is three parts: spirit, soul and body (see 1 Thess. 5:23). Your body is what you can see in the mirror. Your soul is your mind and emotions. Your spirit is the real you that lives inside your body. It is not made of bones or blood, but of spiritual material. It has a shape and form, just like your body. When your body dies, you, as a spirit, will leave your body and go to heaven if you are a follower of Jesus.

It is people's spirits that need to be reborn in order for them to get into God's future kingdom because if a person is not born again, his spirit has a sinful, satanic nature that has no relationship with God. He is spiritually dead. But when a person repents and believes in Jesus, the Holy Spirit comes into his spirit and removes the old sinful nature and gives that person a new nature, making him a child of God. Before a person is born again, the devil is his spiritual father. After he is born again, God is his spiritual Father.

As Jesus said, none of us can see the wind, and neither can we see people's spirits being born again nor the Holy Spirit that makes people's spirits new. However, just as we can see the effects of the wind, for example, leaves moving in the trees, so we can see the effects of the Holy Spirit when He moves inside a person's spirit. When He does, people start loving God and serving Him.

Jesus also explained to Nicodemus what he had to do in order to be born again. He told Nicodemus that He would be lifted up on a pole, meaning the cross, and that anyone who believed in Him would then forever have the new life that the Holy Spirit gives. It was just like the story of Moses and the people of Israel in the desert. One time God became very angry with them because of their sins, so He sent snakes into their camp, and anyone who was bitten, died. Moses prayed for God to have mercy, and so God told Moses to make a snake out of bronze and attach it to a pole. Moses then sent news to the people, "If anyone who is dying from a snake bite will come and look at the bronze snake on the pole, he will live."

The people who believed the news came, looked, and were healed. In the same way, all people have been filled with the venom of sin. Their spirits are dead and their bodies are dying. But if they will believe in the Lord Jesus who hung on the cross, bearing our sins, their dead spirits will be made alive and their bodies will one day live again forever. Have you believed that good news? If you have, you've been born twice! (Maybe you should try to convince your mom that you deserve two birthday parties every year!)

Q. Jesus said that people must be born of "water" as well as the Spirit. What do you think He meant?

A. Different Christians have different answers to that question. Some say Jesus was talking about when a person is born as a baby. When babies are inside their mothers, they are enclosed by a sac of water. Just before they're born, that water sac breaks, so water comes out before the baby does.

A second interpretation is that Jesus was referring to people being baptized. Everyone who believes in Jesus should be baptized in water soon after they first believe. However, you don't have to be baptized in order to be born again. Baptism represents what has already happened the moment a person first believes in Jesus: He was dead but now has come back to life. Being under the water symbolizes being buried, and coming out of the water symbolizes being raised from the dead.

A third interpretation is that water is symbolic for God's Word. Truly, in order to be born again, a person needs to first hear the good news of Jesus' sacrificial death. Then, if he believes it, the Holy Spirit causes his spirit to be born again. People need both the Word of God and the Holy Spirit to be reborn.

Q. We read the most famous verse in the whole New Testament today, John 3:16. It tells us why God gave us His only Son. Why did He?

A. Because He loves us.

Application: *Since our spirits have been born again, we should follow the inward leading of our new nature to obey God, and not the evil leading of the old nature that we also still possess. We're thankful that one day that old sinful nature will be completely done away with when we get brand new bodies.*

NOTES:

Jesus Continues His Conversation with Nicodemus
John 3:17-21

Jesus really wanted Nicodemus to understand how he could have his sins forgiven and be born again. Nicodemus needed to know that salvation is not something that *he could earn* , but something that *was earned for him* by Jesus Christ and is therefore a free gift from God. It is only through Jesus that anyone can be saved. That is why Jesus told Nicodemus that God sent His Son into the world, not to condemn it, but to save it. God wants everyone in the world to be saved because He loves us all.

If God wants every person to be saved, then why isn't everyone saved? The reason is because people have a part to play in their salvation. As Jesus explained to Nicodemus, every person must individually, by himself, believe that Jesus is the Son of God.

But why doesn't everyone believe that Jesus is the Son of God? Jesus explained the answer to that question by using the words *darkness* and *light*. Darkness represents ignorance (which means not knowing the truth). Light is symbolic of knowing the truth. When you turn out the lights in your bedroom at night, you are somewhat ignorant of where things are. You can't see where you're going and might stub your toe on your bed. But when the light is on, you can clearly see your path. Now you know what you didn't know when you were in darkness.

Jesus said that light from heaven came into the world. He was speaking of the truth that He brought from God the Father and shared with people on earth. Jesus said that people love the darkness and hate the light. They stay away from the light. That is, they don't want to know the truth that Jesus brought.

But why don't people want to know the truth? Jesus also explained that. The reason is because people don't want to stop sinning, and they know that if they come to the light and believe the truth, they will have to change the way they live. So they remain in the darkness, purposely believing all kinds of lies from Satan so that they can continue rebelling against God.

That is the reason, for example, that some people believe that there is no God. Even though it is obvious from looking at all God has made that He must exist, people don't want to believe it because they know that if there is a God, He has a right to tell them how to live. They want to control their own lives and keep sinning, so they believe the lie that God doesn't exist.

Thankfully, *some* people come out of the darkness into the light. Those are people who willingly repent of their rebellion against God because they believe the good news that Jesus is the Son of God who freely offers them salvation. This is why it is necessary to repent, or turn away from sin and selfishness, in order to be saved. Repenting of sin doesn't earn us our salvation---but repenting is the proof that we really believe that Jesus is the Son of God.

Some people think they are saved even though they have never repented of sin, but they are mistaken. True Christians, although not perfect, are trying to please God and obey Him. People who are constantly sinning aren't really saved. They are still living in darkness, believing the lie that they can have a relationship with God while they continue a lifestyle of disobedience to Him. They will go to hell when they die. But those who have truly believed in Jesus, as proven by how they live their lives, don't have to worry about going to hell. As Jesus said, "There is no judgment awaiting those who trust" Him (John 3:18).

Q. Nicodemus heard everything he needed to know in order to be saved, but our reading today doesn't tell us if he believed it. Do you think Nicodemus ever "came to the light"?

A. According to other scripture verses, we know that he did. He helped another man, Joseph of Arimathea, bury Jesus' body after He was crucified (see John 19:38-42). By doing so, because he was a ruler and well-known teacher of the Jews, Nicodemus risked being rejected by many people who hated Jesus. But it is better to believe in Jesus and be rejected by others than not to believe in Jesus and be rejected by God and cast into hell!

Application: *Sometimes kids who are raised in Christian homes and who have always been taught to do the right thing have a hard time remembering when they first believed in Jesus and repented of their sins. Perhaps you are one of those kids. If you are, don't let it concern you. The important thing is, do you believe in Jesus right now? And is your faith in Jesus evident by how you live your life? Are you trying to obey God? Perhaps your parents, if they were not raised in a Christian home, can tell you about when they first believed in Jesus and repented.*

NOTES:

John's Final Testimony About Jesus
John 3:22-36

Today we realize even more what a humble man John the Baptist was. We can learn a lot about humility by considering his words and deeds.

Although John was, according to Jesus, the greatest person to have ever lived (see Matthew 11:11), John knew that Jesus was far superior to himself, since Jesus was God from heaven. Pride sneaks into our lives when we compare ourselves with others. If we know we're better at doing something than someone else, we can become prideful. If, however, we will compare ourselves with Jesus, as John did, we won't be able to become proud.

Most often, we compare ourselves with people who have similar abilities and talents. If I'm a basketball player, I don't care how good another person might be at playing the piano---I'm only interested in other basketball players. For a while, John was the most famous preacher around. Multitudes traveled great distances to hear his anointed sermons and to be baptized. But then Jesus started doing the same things as John, preaching and baptizing, and Jesus' popularity began to grow. Additionally, God gave Jesus the Holy Spirit "without measure" (John 3:34), something He didn't do for John. Thus Jesus was able to perform miracles, something John never did, and those miracles really attracted large crowds. God the Father gave Jesus "authority over everything" (John 3:35), including sicknesses and demons. Before long, hardly anyone was coming to hear John, and some of his own disciples became jealous for him.

John, however, realized his place and time in God's plan. His job was to prepare the way for Jesus. The whole idea from the beginning was that *Jesus* would be exalted, not John. John knew his ministry would be temporary and said of Jesus, "He must become greater and greater, and I must become less and less" (John 3:30). Proud people don't want to ever let go of something

God has given them, even when it's obvious that God's plan for them is that they move on to do something else because God has anointed another person to take their place. Proud people want to be recognized and appreciated more and more. Christians, however, should want Jesus to become greater in people's minds, not themselves. They should be interested in building God's kingdom and not kingdoms for themselves. They should want to be servants, not rulers.

John also knew that Jesus was the only way to heaven, and that only Jesus could give eternal life to people who believed in Him. John clearly understood that those who truly believe in Jesus obey Him. John said, "Those who don't *obey* the Son will never experience eternal life, but the wrath of God remains upon them" (John 3:36, emphasis added). This doesn't mean that if we commit a sin that we will go to hell, because no Christian is perfect and we all do sin at times. We know from reading the rest of the New Testament that John was talking about people who *never* obey Jesus, living a lifestyle of sin and selfishness. They are not submitted to Jesus at all, which proves they don't believe in Him.

Q. Could God ever be guilty of the sin of pride?

A. No, it would be impossible for God to think too highly of Himself. When He speaks of His own wonderful attributes, He isn't bragging---He's only telling the truth.

Q. Is there something that you do better than others? (Parents, this would be a good time for you to compliment your kids for things they do well, as they may think they're being proud if they respond.) Could that talent be an inroad for pride? What can you do to keep pride out?

Q. Is it prideful to say, "I'm a good swimmer" if you *are* a good swimmer?

A. No. Pride is having an inflated or unrealistic opinion of yourself. To say that you are a good swimmer when you *are* a good swimmer is simply telling the truth. But, to say that you are the world's best swimmer (unless you are) would be prideful. It's best to talk as little as possible about yourself, your abilities and your accomplishments, because even if you are just telling the truth, some people might think you are pridefully boasting. As the proverb says, "Don't praise yourself; let others do it!" (Proverbs 27:2).

Application: *The Bible says that God humbles those who exalt themselves and exalts those who humble themselves. In which of these two categories do you fall?*

NOTES:

DAY 24
The Bad Samaritan
John 4:1-26

The people who lived in the region of Samaria came from a mixed ancestry of Jews *and* Gentiles. Because of that, the Samaritans were hated by the Jews who considered themselves of purer ancestry, and the Samaritans hated them in return. It was the same as it is today, when people of different races or cultures hate each other only because they're different.

But God isn't prejudiced. He loves everybody, no matter what color their skin is or what language they speak. Today's reading provides additional proof that Jesus was God, because He loved a Samaritan whom an ordinary Jew would have hated. This woman was very surprised when Jesus spoke to her, because usually, Jews didn't even speak to Samaritans!

Jesus told her that if she knew who He was and what He could give her, *she* would have been the one to initiate the conversation, asking Him for some very special water. Obviously, when Jesus offered her living water, He was speaking symbolically of something else. What was it? Let's look at how Jesus described it.

First, it was something that only He could give. It wasn't available from any other source. Second, it was a free gift, not something that could be purchased or earned. Third, like water, it would go inside people, forever satisfying their spiritual thirst. And fourth, when the living water went inside, it would give people eternal life. Jesus must have been speaking about receiving the Holy Spirit and being born again. He was offering the Samaritan woman salvation.

She, however, didn't understand what Jesus was talking about, and she probably began to wonder if He was a little crazy. So she jokingly requested some of His living water so she wouldn't ever be thirsty or have to haul water again from the well to her house.

She was probably thinking to herself, "How can I get away from this oddball?"

But Jesus knew how to make her seriously consider what He was saying. Before she could see her need for a Savior, she had to acknowledge she was a sinner. So Jesus told her to call her husband, and she replied that she didn't have a husband. By telling a partial truth, she was trying to hide a big secret of which she was very ashamed. And that is when Jesus really got her attention, telling her He knew that she had been married and divorced five times and that now she was living with a man who was not her husband. Now she knew she was talking with Somebody special! He must be a prophet to know things about her past, and she wanted to change the subject in a hurry before He began talking about anything else of which she was ashamed! So she quickly brought up a religious question about the proper place to worship.

Jesus downplayed the importance of what was at that time a big dispute between Jews and Samaritans. It doesn't make any difference *where* a person worships. What matters is *how* he worships. Just because a person is worshipping in Jerusalem or at Mount Gerizim doesn't mean his worship is acceptable to God. The important thing is the condition of a person's heart. The only kind of worship that is acceptable and pleasing to God is worship that is done by people who worship "in spirit and in truth" (John 4:23). That is, their worship has to originate from their spirits, or hearts, and it must be sincere, not just a ritual. They worship God with their lives, living obediently to Him all the time. Only people who are born again can worship that way, and that is exactly what this Samaritan woman lacked.

Still hoping to end their conversation, she tried an argument that guilty people have always used to evade their accountability before God: "People will always disagree about religious issues, but someday God will straighten us all out. So there's no sense in us discussing it now." This woman, however, made the mistake of saying that she figured that when the Messiah came, He would explain everything. So Jesus dropped the bomb, telling her that He was the Messiah! And He *was* explaining to her what she needed to know, so she had no more excuses! Now she was faced with the biggest decision of her life, but we'll have to wait for tomorrow to find out what she decided. (This is what is known as a "cliff-hanger devotional"!)

Q. Is it OK for Christians to be prejudiced against people of other races or cultures?

A. No. Christians should reflect the love that God has for all people. Jesus died for everyone, and the greatest act of love we can show anyone is to tell them about Jesus.

Q. Have you ever tried to convince someone of his or her need for Jesus, but, like this Samaritan woman, he or she keeps trying to evade the issues? What did you learn from Jesus about how to deal with people like that?

A. Don't let them direct the conversation onto what is really not important. Keep it centered on two things: their sinfulness and need for a Savior, and the Lord Jesus Christ, who is the only way anyone can be saved.

Application: *Am I a person who worships "in spirit and truth," or am I just a religious person who practices certain rituals? Is worshipping God something I do just because I'm in church, or something I do because I love God with my heart? Is my daily life an act of worship to God?*

NOTES:

Revival in Sychar
John 4:27-42

When Jesus told this woman at the well of Sychar that He was the Messiah, she had to make a decision that everybody must make: to believe or not to believe. We can't be *absolutely* certain from what we've read today, but it seems this woman at the well was convinced that Jesus was the Messiah. Soon after Jesus told her who He was, she left her water jar and went back into her village, telling everyone to come and meet a man who knew her past. "Can this be the Messiah?" she asked them. Perhaps she was sincerely uncertain at that point and wanted to hear the opinions of the people of her village. Or, perhaps she was already convinced about Jesus, and her apparent uncertainty was just a means of wise persuasion by a woman with a bad reputation in her village. Regardless, after Jesus stayed with the people of Sychar for two days, many of them believed that He was the "Savior of the world" (John 4:42). Though they had previously hated all Jews, these Samaritan people now loved a Jewish man who had first loved them.

While the woman was back in her village telling people what had happened to her, Jesus' disciples returned from the village with food. They urged Him to eat something, and, not surprisingly, Jesus saw the opportunity to convey a spiritual lesson. He responded, "No...I have food you don't know about" (John 4:32). They thought someone else had brought Him food, but Jesus was talking about His spiritual hunger being satisfied by doing the will of His Father. Just as they had a physical hunger that could only be satisfied with food, He had a spiritual hunger that could only be satisfied by obedience. And, just as we feel much better after eating a good meal (especially if we were really hungry beforehand), Jesus was enjoying the good feeling that came from sharing God's truth with the woman at the well.

Comparing them to harvesters, Jesus then encouraged His disciples to get involved in telling people the good news of who He was. They didn't need to wait for the harvest to ripen as do those who harvest wheat or apples. Jesus' followers were hired to harvest people, and there are always people who are ready to receive the gospel. When Jesus told His disciples this, they were just minutes away from being crowded by spiritually hungry people from Sychar who would soon be saved!

Q. Is there a spiritual hunger inside of us to do God's will?

A. Yes, if a person is born again, Jesus lives inside him by the Holy Spirit, and Jesus wants to obey God the Father. When we obey God by telling people His truth, we'll get a good feeling on the inside, because our spiritual hunger will be satisfied for a while.

Q. Is leading people to Jesus the only thing that we can do that contributes to the spiritual harvest that God desires?

A. No, Jesus said that some people plant seeds, while others harvest. We can plant seeds by loving unbelievers, living rightly before them and by sharing the good news. Although they might not believe in Jesus immediately, hopefully our good influence will lead to their eventual conversion, even if someone else gets the privilege of actually seeing them repent and become a follower of Christ. However, Jesus said that there is joy awaiting both planters and harvesters. When we get to heaven and see the people there whom we helped come to Christ, we will be very happy!

Application: *We should live our lives in such a way that people are attracted to Jesus. The most important thing that we can do is tell someone else about Jesus.*

NOTES:

Jesus Visits His Hometown
Luke 4:14-30

After spending two days in Sychar (where Jesus met the woman at the well) Jesus and His disciples continued journeying to the region of Galilee. When they arrived, Jesus preached in many places, telling people to repent and believe the good news. He often taught on Saturdays, the Sabbath day of the Jews, in their small church buildings, called synagogues.

One of the places Jesus visited in Galilee was Nazareth, the town in which He had grown up. Because He never sinned, Jesus probably had a good reputation there. However, when He had lived among them, none of His friends or acquaintances realized He was God's Son. He had never told them who He was or worked any miracles. To the people of Nazareth, Jesus was just a good man, a carpenter by trade, one of the five sons of Mary and Joseph (see Matthew 13:55-56; Mark 6:3). Since they had last seen Him, however, He had received the power of the Holy Spirit, and they had heard He was performing miracles in other parts of Galilee. Now it was time for Jesus to tell them who He was, and so He joined the people of Nazareth at their synagogue one Saturday.

On this occasion, Jesus was given the scroll of the book of Isaiah to read before the congregation. He opened it to some verses that described the Messiah's ministry, hoping they would realize that He was the one of whom Isaiah had written. The word *messiah* means "anointed one," and the portion of Isaiah's prophecy from which Jesus read, spoke of a person who would be anointed by God's Spirit to preach, deliver and heal. That is exactly what Jesus had been doing. In fact, the first thing the people of Nazareth noticed was Jesus' ability to speak. They were all "amazed by the gracious words that fell from his lips" (Luke 4:22).

Even though the people of Nazareth had heard the report of His miracles in other towns, most of them refused to believe that one of their hometown boys was the anointed person Isaiah had predicted would come. They wanted to see some miracles right before their eyes before they would believe in Him. Their hearts were hard, and Jesus responded to their unbelief by saying that prophets are usually not received in their hometowns.

Even though Jesus wasn't surprised by their unbelief, He was saddened by it, because He knew it would hinder God's work in their midst. Then He cited two other prophets who weren't received by their own people, and as a result, those people missed out on blessings that other people, even foreigners, enjoyed. Once during the time of Elijah the prophet, there was a three-and-one-half year famine in Israel. Jesus said that there were many Israelite widows who suffered during that famine, but God sent Elijah only to a foreign widow to provide food supernaturally for her. And during the time of the prophet Elisha, there were many Israelites who needed to be healed of leprosy, but God used Elisha to heal only one leper, and he also was a foreigner.

Jesus' message to the people of Nazareth was clear: because they rejected Him, an anointed man of God and the Messiah, they would forfeit God's blessing, just like the Israelites of Elijah and Elisha's day. When the people in the synagogue realized what Jesus was saying, their mood quickly changed. At the beginning of His sermon, "all who were there spoke well of him" (Luke 4:22). By the end of His sermon, they wanted to kill Him, revealing the wickedness within their hearts. As they often do, desires turned into deeds, and they attempted to kill Him by throwing Him over a cliff. Jesus, however, was somehow supernaturally delivered. Perhaps God the Father made Him temporarily invisible! Wouldn't that be fun if God did that to you?

Q. According to the Bible, Jesus had four younger brothers and at least two younger sisters. He knows what it is like to live as part of a family. What kind of an older brother do you think Jesus was?

A. He was the *perfect* older brother! That means He always thought first of His younger brothers and sisters before thinking of Himself. He assisted them whenever they needed His help and shared with them what was His. Because Jesus lives in you by the Holy Spirit, you have the potential to be the kind of brother (or sister) that Jesus was as He grew up.

Q. Just as the people who knew Jesus before He was anointed by the Holy Spirit found it difficult to believe that He was the Messiah, often the people who knew us before we were born again by God's Spirit have a difficult time believing that we've been changed. What is the best way to convince them that you're not the person they knew before?

A. By our daily lives. As they listen to us and observe our actions, they'll see that we've changed. Then they'll be more open to hearing the good news about Jesus.

Application: *People who reject Jesus reject God's blessings. Because we believe in Jesus, God is going to bless us forever!*

NOTES:

Jesus Demonstrates His Authority Over Evil Spirits and Sickness
Mark 1:21-39

For a while Jesus lived in Capernaum, a village on the coast of the Sea of Galilee, and He frequently taught in the synagogue there. The people who heard Him were amazed at His teaching because He taught "as one who had real authority" (Mark 1:22). That means Jesus came across as if He was absolutely certain of what He was saying. This is another proof that Jesus was God in the form of a human being. Naturally, God knows what He is talking about. Jesus never said, "I may be wrong, but let Me tell you how I feel about that subject" or, "Your opinion is as good as Mine." If He had said those things, we'd know He really wasn't God.

Once, right as Jesus was teaching in the synagogue in Capernaum, a man who was possessed by an evil spirit began shouting at Him. The evil spirit was actually the one speaking, using the man's mouth, and he said, "Why are you bothering us, Jesus of Nazareth? Have you come to destroy us? I know who you are-the Holy One sent from God!" (Mark 1:24). Jesus, to whom God the Father had given authority over everything, including evil spirits (see John 3:35), commanded the evil spirit to come out of the man, and it did. From this incident, we can learn several things about Jesus and evil spirits.

If you're born again, you don't have to worry about evil spirits getting inside you or possessing you, because Jesus lives inside you by the Holy Spirit. This man who was possessed by an evil spirit wasn't born again. The Bible tells us, "The [Holy] Spirit who lives in you is greater than the spirit who lives in the world [the devil]" (1 John 4:4). Evil spirits are no match for Jesus. The evil spirit we just read about was afraid that Jesus was going to completely destroy him and all his fellow evil spirits.

This evil spirit also knew who Jesus was, calling Him "the Holy One sent from God" (Mark 1:24). Evil spirits like to brag about what they know, but in doing so, this particular demon showed how stupid he was. He said something in the synagogue that his boss, the devil, didn't want *anyone* to know! I wonder if he got in trouble with the devil for shooting off his mouth!

Regardless, when the demon-possessed man was delivered, the news spread quickly in Galilee. God the Father was advertising His Son because He wanted people to listen to what Jesus was telling them. Believing Jesus' message was the only way people could have their sins forgiven.

Next we read about Jesus healing Peter's mother-in-law who had a very high fever. The news of that miracle also spread quickly, and when evening arrived, many sick and demon-possessed people came to Peter and Andrew's house seeking help. According to Matthew and Luke's Gospels, Jesus healed and delivered every single one of them (see Matthew 8:16; Luke 4:40-41). This not only again proves that Jesus was the Messiah sent from God, it also shows us that Jesus loves everyone who is sick or possessed by evil spirits. He loves them enough to heal and deliver them.

Q. In the final verses of our reading today, we read that Jesus arose early in the morning and went out into the wilderness to pray. Why would God need to pray? What do you think Jesus prayed about?

A. While Jesus was on earth, He was following His Father's orders. One reason He prayed was to receive those orders. From what we read today about Jesus' prayer time, it seems He received direction to leave Capernaum to preach in other towns (see Mark 1:38).

Q. We know that no true Christian could be possessed by a demon. But why is it that only *some* unsaved people become possessed by demons?

A. No one knows for sure. However, it is quite likely that many unsaved people who become demon-possessed open the door to possession by continually thinking wrong thoughts and giving in to temptation. An evil spirit can't get inside any person it wants. Becoming demon-possessed is normally a gradual, progressive thing that begins when a person yields to the suggestions of a demon.

Application: *Just as elephants shouldn't be afraid of mice, we shouldn't be afraid of the devil and evil spirits. They're afraid of Jesus who lives in us!*

NOTES:

Jesus Heals a Man With Leprosy
Mark 1:40-45

If you live in the United States or any other developed nation, you will probably never see a person with leprosy. It's a horrible skin disease that actually eats away at the parts of the body it has infected. People who are afflicted with leprosy watch their fingers and toes slowly dissolve. Eventually, they die from the disease. To make matters worse, leprosy is easily spread to other people, so no one wants to be near a leper. When a person gets leprosy, he soon loses all his friends. In the Old Testament, God made a law that required all leprous people to cry out, "Unclean! Unclean!" whenever they were in a public place where other people might be infected (see Leviticus 13:45).

The Greek word translated *leprosy* was used to describe various skin diseases in Jesus' time, so it's possible that this man whom Jesus healed was not suffering from the disease we refer to today as leprosy. However, there's no doubt he had a very serious physical problem, and his situation was desperate. He fell on his knees before Jesus, begging to be healed. From the reports he had heard of others being healed, he knew Jesus was *able* to cure him. But he didn't know if Jesus *wanted* to heal him. Jesus, however, was moved with pity for the distraught man, and assured him that He did want to heal him. A second later, the leprous man felt something he hadn't felt in a long time: the touch of another person. As Jesus put His hand on him, instantly his leprosy was gone. Imagine how he felt as he looked at his new skin!

Some people think that Jesus healed people only to prove that He was the Son of God. Certainly Jesus' healings did prove that. Because God the Father had given Him authority over all things, including disease, Jesus simply spoke and the leprous man was instantly healed. We read today, however, that Jesus was "moved with pity" over the leprous man's situation. Jesus healed this man because He loved him, not just to prove that He was the Son of God.

For *all* Christians, this healing story, along with the many others in the Bible, affirms that God cares about our health and will one day give us brand new bodies that will not be subject to sickness and disease. For *some* Christians, like myself, the stories of people whom Jesus healed inspire us to trust that we don't have to wait until heaven to experience physical healing. Jesus never told anyone who came to Him requesting healing, "Rejoice, because in heaven you'll be healthy." In every case, He healed sick people, often crediting their faith. When we remain ill, we often claim that it must not be God's will for us to be healed, but more likely, our own lack of faith is to blame. Jesus said, "Anything is possible if a person believes" (Mark 9:23). Praise God that we can trust God for healing, and praise God that even if we fail to trust God for healing, He doesn't condemn us.

According to the Old Testament law, the priests were responsible to determine whether or not people had leprosy. If a person thought he might have contracted the disease, he was supposed to be examined by a priest. If the priest declared him a leper, he had to obey the laws of leprosy, removing himself from contact with non-leprous society. Likewise, if a leprous person was healed, only a priest could make the official determination and allow the former leper reentry into normal society.

Jesus commanded this leper to obey that law and show himself to the priest, taking along the required offering, as a testimony of his healing. It was probably the first time that priest ever performed that part of his job, declaring a leper to be cleansed! I wonder if he had to look up the appropriate scriptures just to find out what he was supposed to do!

Q. Why did Jesus tell this man He healed not to talk to anyone on his way to the priest?

A. Because Jesus didn't need any more advertising. If the former leper started spreading the news of what happened, Jesus knew He would soon be mobbed with people, and it would actually hinder His ministry. Sure enough, the man didn't obey Jesus, telling everyone what had happened, and Jesus was then unable to publicly enter any nearby towns. Several days later, Jesus did sneak back into Capernaum where He had been living, but was soon discovered. Within a short time, the house where He was staying was crammed with people, inside and out (see Mark 2:1-4).

Q. Wouldn't it be horrible never to be touched by anyone? Sometimes parents feel like they must have leprosy, because their kids never hug or kiss them (especially when their kids are with friends). Have you hugged your parents today?

Application: *In one way, we were like this leper. We had a spiritual disease that prevented us from ever hoping to enter the society of heaven. But Jesus cleansed us! Now we can look forward to enjoying eternal life with the many others like us whom Jesus has cleansed of sin.*

NOTES:

DAY 29

Jesus Heals a Paralyzed Man
Mark 2:1-12

Can you imagine what it would have been like to witness this miracle? Four men brought their paralyzed friend on a pallet to a house where they heard Jesus was staying. Upon arrival, they discovered that the house was jammed with people, and many others were standing outside looking in, blocking all the doors and windows. There was no way to get their friend close to Jesus.

But they would not be discouraged. The roofs of the houses in Capernaum were flat, and many of them had stairs that went from the outside of the house up to the roof. So they carried their paralyzed friend to the roof of the house, dug an opening through the clay, and then lowered him on his pallet by ropes right in front of Jesus. It must have taken a lot of time and effort to dig through the hardened clay roof and caused some commotion inside the house when the clay dust began falling from the ceiling. I wonder what the people inside were thinking as they coughed, wiped dust from their eyes, and watched a hole slowly form in the ceiling above their heads.

What was Jesus thinking then? He was thinking about the faith of the men who were going to so much trouble. The Bible says that it is "impossible to please God without faith" (Hebrews 11:6). Because of their faith, the paralyzed man was forgiven and completely healed within seconds. If they hadn't believed, they would never have gone to so much trouble, and their friend would have remained un-forgiven and paralyzed, even though it was obviously God's will for the man to be forgiven and healed.

Why did Jesus first tell the paralyzed man that his sins were forgiven? No one knows for sure, but perhaps the paralyzed man was coming to Jesus both for healing *and* forgiveness. Certainly being forgiven of sins is even more important than being healed. Or, perhaps the paralyzed man, because of all his sins, had doubts that he would be healed, so Jesus removed his doubts by assuring him of forgiveness. Or, possibly the man had become paralyzed as a direct result of some sin he had committed. In that case, Jesus took care of the cause before giving the cure.

Regardless, when Jesus told him that his sins were forgiven, it caused quite a stir among the religious teachers who were present. They knew that only God could forgive sins, so Jesus was claiming to be God! They thought He was guilty of blasphemy (saying something that was very offensive to God).

Jesus knew what the religious teachers were thinking, so He proved, right before their eyes, that He had the right to forgive sins, also proving His deity. Anyone could pretend to have the authority to forgive sins because there would be no visible result. But no one can convincingly pretend to have authority to heal paralysis, because the result would be plain for everyone to see. When Jesus instantly healed the paralyzed man, it proved He had authority to heal, and it gave credibility to His claim to be able to forgive sins.

To us, this is one more proof that Jesus was the Son of God. If an average sinful human being claimed to be able to forgive sins, we would know he was blaspheming. But when a virgin-born, sinless, miracle-working person forgives someone's sins, it's just one more proof of what we would already suspect: God had become a man!

Q. We read that Jesus actually *saw* the faith of the four men and their paralyzed friend. How can faith be seen?

A. By actions. The Bible says, "faith is dead without good deeds" (James 2:26). Many people say that they believe in Jesus, but only those who have corresponding actions really do. Sometimes, Christians say they believe certain promises in the Bible, but their contrary actions prove that they really don't.

Q. Just like this man whom Jesus healed, our sins have been forgiven by Jesus. If we truly believe our sins are forgiven, we will act like forgiven people. How do forgiven people act?

A. At the minimum, they would be happy and grateful to God for their forgiveness, and would show their gratitude by obedience to God.

Application: *There has never been another person in history like Jesus. Other people in history may have claimed to forgive sins, but their lives proved they were phony. Any honest person who examines the evidence will be convinced that Jesus was God in the form of a human being.*

NOTES:

Jesus Dines with Matthew and His Sinful Friends
Luke 5:27-32

Apparently Levi, also known as Matthew, had been touched by
Jesus' ministry in Capernaum. Perhaps he had listened as Jesus
taught by the Sea of Galilee or heard the testimonies of people
who had been healed. When Jesus called Matthew to be His
disciple, he didn't hesitate for a minute, but left everything behind
to follow his new Lord.

What was so amazing about Matthew's calling is that he was a
very sinful man---at least until he met Jesus. Matthew was a tax
collector, which meant that he worked for Rome, the country that
occupied and controlled Israel at that time. The Israelites hated the
Romans, and naturally they had no respect for any fellow Israelite
who worked for them. Tax collectors were considered traitors by
their countrymen.

Beyond that, tax collectors had a reputation for being very
dishonest, forcing their fellow Israelites to pay more in taxes than
Rome required and then keeping the extra money for themselves.
In so doing, they became rich at the expense of their own
neighbors. Thus, the only type of people who would have been
Matthew's friends were fellow tax collectors and other people of
very low moral character. Those were the type of people who
came to Matthew's banquet.

Matthew, however, had become a disciple of Jesus, repenting of
his sins, and as is the case of anyone who is a true follower of
Jesus, he wanted his friends to meet Jesus also and be saved. That
is the reason he held a banquet in Jesus' honor. It was a low-key
evangelistic meeting, and Jesus, who loves everyone, gladly
accepted the invitation to spend some time eating with Matthew's
sinful friends.

Because He did, He was criticized by the Pharisees and religious teachers, who would never associate with such people. Jesus responded by informing them that the purpose of His coming was to "call sinners to turn from their sins" (Luke 5:32). In order to do that, He had to spend time with sinners, and that is exactly why He attended Matthew's banquet. Jesus didn't spend His time at that banquet talking about sports or the weather! He was telling sinners that they needed to repent and follow Him, just as their friend Matthew had!

Q. The Pharisees and religious teachers we read about today didn't understand two important things. First, they thought holy people shouldn't associate with sinful people. But just the opposite is true. If people are *truly* holy, they *will* associate with sinful people, because holy people are motivated by love to share Jesus with those who need to be saved.

That should give you a clue concerning the second thing about which the Pharisees and religious teachers were mistaken. What was it?

A. They thought they were holy, but actually they were themselves sinners who needed to be saved. Jesus referred to this fact when He said, "I have come to call sinners to turn from their sins, not to spend my time with *those who think they are already good enough* " (Luke 5:32, emphasis added). Jesus was speaking of the Pharisees and religious teachers.

Q. What would you think if your pastor accepted an invitation to a party that was hosted by a newly-converted drug pusher for his drug pusher friends?

Application: *Jesus in us loves evil and sinful people. Do we? Or are we like the Pharisees who considered themselves too holy to spend time with sinners?*

NOTES

Our prayer is that you have been blessed by spending 30 days with your family and more importantly, with God and His word. Please continue with your family devotions. Go to **http://www.heavensfamily.org/ss/devotionals** or to **www.manupgodsway.org** to download 117 more days for you and your family. We know you and your family will be blessed.

God bless and share your faith,

Jody Burkeen
Man Up! Gods Way
Burkeen Ministries Inc.

27583872R10050

Made in the USA
Columbia, SC
26 September 2018